IT'S SNOWY

Written by
Azra Limbada

Published in 2023 by **KidHaven Publishing,** **an Imprint of Greenhaven Publishing, LLC**
29 East 21st Street
New York, NY 10010

© 2020 Booklife Publishing
This edition is published by arrangement with Booklife Publishing

Edited by: William Anthony

Designed by: Chris Cooper

Cataloging-in-Publication Data

Names: Limbada, Azra.
Title: It's snowy / Azra Limbada.
Description: New York : KidHaven Publishing, 2023. | Series: What's the weather? | Includes glossary and index.
Identifiers: ISBN 9781534540699 (pbk.) | ISBN 9781534540712 (library bound) | ISBN 9781534540705 (6 pack) | ISBN 9781534540729 (ebook)
Subjects: LCSH: Snow--Juvenile literature. | Weather--Juvenile literature.
Classification: LCC QC926.37 L536 2023 | DDC 551.57'84--dc23

All rights reserved. No part of this book may be reproduced in any form without permission in writing from the publisher, except by a reviewer.

Manufactured in the United States of America

CPSIA compliance information: Batch #CSKH23: For further information contact Greenhaven Publishing LLC, New York, New York at 1-844-317-7404.

Please visit our website, www.greenhavenpublishing.com. For a free color catalog of all our high-quality books, call toll free 1-844-317-7404 or fax 1-844-317-7405.

Find us on

PHOTO CREDITS

All images are courtesy of Shutterstock.com, unless otherwise specified. With thanks to Getty Images, Thinkstock Photo and iStockphoto. Front Cover – Echunder, A3pfamily, Mike Mareen, Evgeny Atamanenko, Libor Fousek. Character throughout – yusufdemirci. 4 – By Aluca69. 5 – Creative Travel Projects. 7 – Carlos Horta. 8 – Sunny Forest. 9 – Tita77. 10–11 – Sthapana Sriyingyong. 12 – Triff. 13 – Jefunne. 14 – Evgeny Bakharev, yusufdemirci. 15 – Bobkov Evgeniy, cuppucino. 16 – Ipedan. 17 – bibiphoto. 18 – Delbars. 19 – Gecko1968. 20 – Smit. 21 – Max Topchii. 22 – Barbara_Krupa. 23 – aleksandr4300.

CONTENTS

Page 4	What Can You See?
Page 6	Seasons
Page 8	It's Snowing!
Page 10	The Water Cycle
Page 12	Up in the Clouds
Page 14	Snowflakes
Page 16	Blizzard!
Page 18	Animals
Page 20	Snow Fun
Page 22	Melting Away
Page 24	Glossary and Index

Words that look like <u>this</u> can be found in the glossary on page 24.

WHAT CAN YOU SEE?

Take a look outside. What can you see? Are the trees swooshing in the wind or is there a big rainbow in the sky?

Weather is what you can see in the sky and feel in the air outside. There are many types of weather, such as rain, sunshine, wind, and snow.

Hi! I'm Snowy the Snowball.

SEASONS

Winter

Spring

Autumn

Summer

In many places, there are four seasons every year. They are called spring, summer, autumn, and winter. Each season has different kinds of weather.

Winter is the season when everything gets very cold. This means you will have to dress in warm clothes before going outside.

You might even get to make me!

IT'S SNOWING!

Look at all the snow covering the winter forest!

Snow may fall from the sky when the weather is very cold. Snow is made up of lots of tiny ice crystals.

If the <u>temperature</u> is cold enough, the snow will fall as powder. This means it will cover the ground like a big white blanket.

Snow angels

Brrr! Can you make snow angels too?

THE WATER CYCLE

The water on our planet never goes away. We always have the same amount of water on Earth. It moves around in a big <u>cycle</u>.

I am part of the water cycle!

When the sunlight heats water up, some of it rises into the sky.
It cools down and makes clouds.

UP IN THE CLOUDS

All the fluffy clouds that you see in the sky are made of air and lots of tiny <u>droplets</u> of water.

When the temperature is at <u>freezing point</u> or below, the water droplets in the clouds stick together to make little snowflakes.

I am made from lots of tiny ice crystals!

SNOWFLAKES

Snow may fall from clouds like these.

The little snowflakes will keep getting bigger until they are too heavy to stay in the sky. That's when they fall down from the clouds.

BLIZZARD!

Look at how much snow there is!

A blizzard is when certain types of cold weather come together to make a <u>storm</u>. Blizzards are made up of strong winds and lots of heavy snow.

This car is trying to drive through a blizzard.

Blizzards are very dangerous. They can make it hard to see. Because a blizzard happens when it is very cold, you can get <u>frostbite</u> if you are outside in one for too long.

ANIMALS

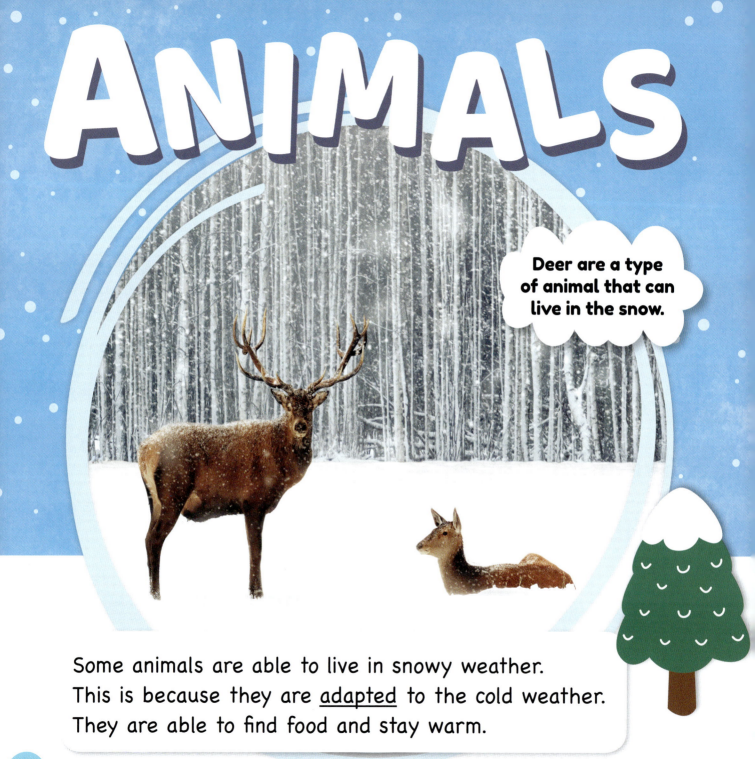

Deer are a type of animal that can live in the snow.

Some animals are able to live in snowy weather. This is because they are <u>adapted</u> to the cold weather. They are able to find food and stay warm.

Polar bears live in the snowy Arctic. Their thick fur helps them to stay warm and blend in with the snow.

This mother polar bear and her cub love playing in the snow!

SNOW FUN

Playing in the snow can be lots of fun. Some children make snowmen and dress them in hats and scarves. Children may also go skiing.

It is important to dress warmly and play safely in the snow, even if you are just throwing snowballs at each other!

Wear a helmet to stay safe when skiing, sledding, or throwing snowballs.

MELTING AWAY

The sunlight has melted this snow.

As the weather gets warmer, snow melts away and turns back into water. Some of the water seeps into the ground and helps plants grow.

Some of the water goes back into the sky. It makes new clouds and becomes part of the water cycle again.

Watch me disappear into the air and become a new cloud!

GLOSSARY

adapted	able to exist in a certain environment because of changes that have happened over time
cycle	a set of events that happen again and again in the same order
droplets	very small drops of liquid, such as water
freezing point	the temperature at which water turns to ice, which is 32 degrees Fahrenheit or 0 degrees Celsius
frostbite	when very cold weather freezes and hurts the skin
ice crystals	small shapes made of frozen water
storm	strong weather such as heavy rain and wind
temperature	how hot or cold something is

INDEX

blizzards 16–17
clothes 7, 20–21
clouds 11–14, 23
crystals 8, 13
droplets 12–13
ice 8, 13
melting 22–23
people 7, 9, 17, 20–21
snowflakes 13–15
storms 16
sunlight 5, 11, 22
water 10–13, 22–23